# TELLING TALES

Patience Agbabi was born in London in 1965 and educated at Oxford and Sussex Universities. She has performed her poetry live, on TV and radio all over the world. Her work has also appeared on the London Underground and human skin. She has lectured in Creative Writing at several UK universities including Greenwich, Cardiff and Kent, and is currently Fellow in Creative Writing at Oxford Brookes University. She was Canterbury Laureate from 2009 to 2010. *Telling Tales* is her fourth poetry collection. She lives in Kent with her husband and two children.

'An energetic compendium of familiar stories translated into the contemporary idiom of street slang and slam poetry'
*Times Literary Supplement*

'Patience Agbabi's *Telling Tales* is a brilliant, virtuosic take on Chaucer's *Canterbury Tales* as spoken by a dazzling list of contemporary characters . . . If *Telling Tales* is not one of the books of the year or in line for a major prize it will be proof the world has grown very dull indeed. This is a landmark book that extends the domain of poetry'
George Szirtes

'*Telling Tales* is a carefully constructed wonder tour. Agbabi is a genius. And this is her best work yet'
Lemn Sissay

# TELLING TALES

## PATIENCE AGBABI

**CANONGATE**

*Edinburgh · London*

This edition published in 2015 by Canongate Books

First published in Great Britain in 2014 by
Canongate Books Ltd, 14 High Street, Edinburgh EH1 1TE

www.canongate.tv

1

*British Library Cataloguing-in-Publication Data*

A catalogue record for this book is available on request from the British Library

ISBN: 978 1 78211 157 3

Typeset in Baskerville MT by Palimpsest Book Production Ltd, Falkirk, Stirlingshire

Printed and bound in Great Britain by Clays Ltd, St Ives plc

*... Whoso shal telle a tale after a man,*
*He moot reherce as ny as evere he kan*
*Everich a word, if it be in his charge,*
*Al speke he never so rudeliche and large,*
*Or ellis he moot telle his tale untrewe,*
*Or feyne thyng, or fynde wordes newe.*

Geoffrey Chaucer

# Contents

# TELLING TALES

# Prologue (Grime Mix)

Harry 'Bells' Bailey

When my April showers me with kisses
I could make her my missus or my mistress
but I'm happily hitched – sorry home girls –
said my vows to the sound of the Bow Bells
yet her breath is as fresh as the west wind,
when I breathe her, I know we're predestined
to make music; my muse, she inspires me,
though my mind's overtaxed, April fires me,
how she pierces my heart to the fond root
till I bleed sweet cherry blossom en route
to our bliss trip; there's days she goes off me,
April loves me not; April loves me
with a passion, dear doctor, I'm wordsick
and I got the itch like I'm allergic
but it could be my shirt's on the cheap side;
serenade overnight with my peeps wide,
nothing like her, liqueur, an elixir,
overproof that she serves as my sick cure,
she's as strong as a ram, she is Aries,
see my jaw-dropping jeans, she could wear these;
see my jaw dropping neat Anglo-Saxon,
I got ink in my veins more than Caxton
and it flows hand to mouth, here's a mouthfeast,
verbal feats from the streets of the South-East
but my April, she blooms every shire's end,
fit or vint, rich or skint, she inspires *them*
from the grime to the clean-cut iambic,
rime royale, rant or rap, get your slam kick.

1

On this Routemaster bus, get cerebral,
Tabard Inn to Canterbury Cathedral,
poet pilgrims competing for free picks,
Chaucer Tales, track by track, here's the remix
from below-the-belt base to the topnotch;
I won't stop all the clocks with a stopwatch
when the tales overrun, run offensive,
or run clean out of steam, they're authentic
cos we're keeping it real, reminisce this:
Chaucer Tales were an unfinished business.
May the best poet lose, as the saying goes.
May the best poet muse be mainstaying those
on the stage, on the page, on their subject:
me and April, *we're* The Rhyming Couplet.
I'm The Host for tonight, Harry Bailey,
if I'm tongue-tied, April will bail me,
I'm MC but the M is for mistress
when my April shows me what a kiss is ...

# OLD KENT ROAD

OLD KENT ROAD

# Emily
Robert Knightley

*In Chaucer's story there are two heroes, who are practically indistinguishable from each other, and a heroine, who is merely a name.*

— J R Hulbert

Arc? Dead. And if you're sniffing for his body
you won't find nothing: ransack the Big Smoke
from Bow to Bank. Arc fell for Emily
ten feet deep … I'm Pal, Emily's alter.
Think ego. Arc and me, we shared a cell
for months, it was a shrine to her, a temple.

I miss him, like a gun to the temple.
Too close. Two men locked in a woman's body,
her messed-up head. When I say shared a cell
I'm talking brain. *She* became *us*. Arc smoked
the Romeos, and me, I smoked all tars,
we breathed out on her name, ah! Emily.
Blonde with blacked out highlights Emily.
Our host, the goddess. Looks are temporal.
Who reads her diagnosis? It don't alter
the facts. She made me up to guard her body
from predators, the silhouettes in smoke.
It's when she wears the hourglass and plays damsel,
she lets *me* out. It messes with their brain cells,
my voice, her face. All men want Emily,
they think they have a right. It don't mean smoke.
She acts like growing up was Shirley Temple
and don't remember nothing, but her body

5

knows what happened happened on that altar.
Think bed … Arc's dead. Broke his parole, an alter
crazy on id, he starved us all to cancel
me out for good. It's written off, our body.
He fought to win: I fought for Emily.
I'm dead beat, but I won up here, the temple,
the messed-up head. Sent her a ring, of smoke.

Having a big fat Romeo to smoke
don't make you Winston Churchill. Arc was altered.
He won the war but lost the plot. The temple
became his tomb. And me, I got the damsel.
She don't know yet. We're stitched up, Emily,
one and the same, one rough-cut mind, one body …

*Must've blacked out … This body ain't no temple*
*but what's the alternative, a padded cell?*
*Got anything to smoke? … I'm Emily …*

# The Kiss
Robyn Miller

Get me a pint of Southwark piss!
It all took place in a pub like this.
My tongue is black as licorice,
my tale is blue an it goes like this:

I'm just eighteen an newly wed.
My husband's old an crap in bed,
my lover's fit, well hung, well read,
his rival's mad, a musclehead.

Three loves I have an two are thick:
My husband John's a jealous prick,
the rival, Abs, thinks with his dick.
My lover's French, il s'appelle Nick,

in his final year at Greenwich,
Engineering Astrophysics,
he's proposed but I'm a bitch,
I'd leave my husband, but he's rich.

A carpenter, an 'ancient oak'
with a heart tattoo, a real bloke's bloke,
crashed out on what he thought was coke
an fifteen pints of ale. Nick's joke.

# THE MILLER'S TALE

John owns the pub. We live upstairs
an every night he says his prayers,
while Nick, our lodger, flirts downstairs,
where Abs, our bouncer, sells his wares.

This Abs comes on to guys *and* girls.
He pushes weights an class A pills.
Grey eyes, blond hair with baby curls
an a bod as hard as the drugs he sells.

He buys me wine, real ales an Pimms.
He likes his women weasel slim
with eyebrows plucked till they're pencil thin.
His gear is class: I put up with him.

But Nick's more subtle, tweets an texts,
no kiss-me-quick with a pint of Becks.
*Belle femme, je t'aime*, he says, an necks
those pills Abs recommends for sex.

Three men walk into a pub like this
but only one can kiss the kiss.
What is it makes my bottle fizz?
Je ne sais quoi my arse, hear this:

What's in a kiss? I'll kiss an tell.
My husband's kiss is Southwark ale,
my lover's 'baiser', 'fuck' in braille
an I'm his fucked-up femme fatale.

So John's upstairs an proper pissed.
I'm in the bar with Nick. We've kissed
in English, French an every lisped
linguistic twist, you get the gist.

High on the pills that kick like tabs,
we crawl around the floor like crabs,
Adam, Eve, on hormone jabs,
we got The Knowledge like black cabs.

Nous faisons l'amour all night,
an by six o'clock it's still not light
when Abs knocks on the window, tight,
*Kiss me, babes.* I say, *Alright.*

Window's open, total geared
he's tongueing me but something's weird:
too right, cos I ain't got no beard,
stead of my lips, he got my rear!

*Fuck you!* Storms off down the alleyway.
Then tap, tap, tap on the central bay,
Mr Am-I-straight-or-gay?
back for his petit déjeuner!

*À moi!* Nick winks, bares his behind
for Abs's probing lips to find:
then farts a fart, the deadly kind,
a blast that almost makes Abs blind!

We laugh, but Abs laughs last, the sod,
Abs has a hard-on, like his bod,
he grabs Nick's arse, I swear to God,
in goes his red-hot iron rod!

*Bordel de merde!* Well sick, that kiss
cos Abs is built like an obelisk.
John wakes, falls headlong, slips a disc,
slurs, *What in great God's name is this?*

My husband's so in shock to see
the men, he sobers instantly
an doesn't even notice me
until I'm dressed. So I'm Scot-free

but Abs an Nick, he throws them out.
It's made him even more devout.
Now, when I see them, *Kiss?* I shout,
raise my eyebrows high, an pout.

So, I got fucked; John's a fuck*wit*;
an Nick my lover, fucked to shit;
an Abs scored hard, he's fucking fit;
both men were fucked by the fucked-off git.

If you drink your beer in a tulip glass
an kiss the air cos you think you're class
but draw the line at this French farce,
bon appétit – French-kiss my arse!

# Tit for Tat
Ozymandia Reeves

Retro-Glasto-Dogs-on-String:
I'm *Bad* Dog, me, with dykes on speed,
musky, milky, masculine,
Butch Al, Fem Jen and Little Weed
pitch Magic Mushroom, down some mead,
and Weed were whizzing, off her tits,
*Gimmegrassordieyoushits!*

Off we sped in sniff of grass
from Psycho's Psychedelic Plants:
he guards wife, bairn and Moll, his lass,
with Stanley Knife in underpants.
With boxer nose and bulldog stance,
sells dried-out lawn as Purple Haze
but stoned, he'd share whole spliff with gays.

Women's Lib stands for libido!
Fist in air, a Goldsmith First,
our Al; our Jen, a Frida Kahlo
femme with fist to outshake Hirst;
best mates, they oil and lock my fur,
I'm in good hands, me, sniffer dog,
laid off, *Bad* Dog, for sniffing drugs.

I scent the gorgeous and grotesque
at mudbath where all hips hang out.
There's Mrs Psycho, Rubenesque,
her six-month bairn; I roll about,
Dog's paradise, I want for nowt.
There's Molly, *Venus at her Mudbath*.
Psycho, sober, on the warpath …

Tent? More yurt, is Psycho's yard.
They tie me up outside front porch,
sweet smell of Purple, I keep guard,
bark twice to rate this grass top notch.
Psycho bags up. Like hawks, they watch.
Keep cash, while he leaves tent for change,
tugs at knot that keeps me chained

and I'm unleashed! I'm off, *Bad Dog
Seeks Dirty Bitch* for fun blind date
but don't let cat out of the bag
to dykes, I've not come out as straight …
They find me fields away, gone eight,
no strings attached, up to no good,
drag me through seven field of mud

back for grass (now switched for grass).
A Psycho spliff … their heads, their feet
turn Alice-Through-the-Looking-Glass
till Psycho offers bite to eat
and feeds me scraps of veggie meat.
Dykes guess he freed me, swapped our batch:
Psycho beware, you've met your match!

*Sleep*, they slur. Three blow-up bed:
dykes first; Psycho and spouse take next,
bairn's cot stands at end of bed;
Molly takes third. But I smell sex
and Dog in dark has X-ray specs ...
While Psycho and his wife snore phlegm
like philharmonic, Al pokes Jen:

*Got an itch I gotta scratch!*
I noted way she eyed that lass,
no psychedelic psychopath
will stop Butch Al when high on hash,
she's on that Molly in a flash
who's up for owt and understands
and yields like putty in her hands ...

And look at Jen, our lump of lead!
The wife gets up to piss, Jen grins
and moves bairn's cot to foot *their* bed.
So on way back, wife bangs her shin,
confused, she mounts *their* bed, gets in:
Jen mounts her, wrists her, hard and deep,
mad as a dog while Psycho sleeps!

Still dark, when Al yawns, stretches, wakes.
Moll tells her that our dope were muddled.
*I swapped it back, made cosmic cakes.*
*Check the porch.* Then, one last cuddle,
Al gropes round for cot, befuddled,
jumps inside the cotless blow-up,
pulling Psycho's earlobe. *Wake up!*

*Three times I've gloved up Psycho's lass*
*whilst you've been having purple dreams.*
Psycho roars, pull out his cutlass,
missus hears him shouting, screams,
*Si, there's a man on top of me!*
Meaning Jen. Grabs Shepton Mallet
in pitch dark and raises it,

strikes down on what she thinks is Jen,
and hits her husband! Jen and Al
grab dope, the space cakes, t-shirts, jeans
and me – I leave a parting growl –
and run through site, au naturel,
to tent to tell our saga of
free food, free dope, free cakes, free love.

# Roving Mic
Roger of Ware

Roger on the mic,
host, take a hike,
bards, on yer bike …
used ta have acne
worked in a factory
till the boss sacked me,
now I'm the chef
of a city caf
but the riffraff
don't get a look in
if they don't book in.
*Roger, what's cooking?*
Here's what I'm spitting
out of my kitchen
hot and hard-hitting
none of it written.
Rhymes rough and raw
weeping like a sore
bruised and ruptured
rude, interrupted,
but if you lick the spit
you'll get a taste for it …
If you can't flow, sing,
this mic is roving
passed like a baton
till it gets spat on …
First up, The Reveller,
raves like a traveller,

he can tell a tale
for a yard of ale,
cunning linguistics
vital statistics
of the cash he owes
and the blondes he knows
every time he flows.
So put your hands together,
let's hear it for The Reveller ...

Girls say I look Italian
I wear a gold medallion
they ride me like a stallion:
bet on me daily
Kirsty and Kayley
Kylie and Hayley
Millie and Mai Li.
I have fun and games
remembering their names
but cos they sound the same
they never notice when
I cheer another femme
when I'm on top of them.
Talking of horses
bets and racecourses
cards and casinos
ask H if she knows
if they pawned my phone,
waiting on a loan,
crashed on my credits
dashed on my debits,

lend me fifty quid
won't ya jelly squid,
Kylie'll lend me
she owes me plenty
for her boob job
cost a few bob
what a huge flop,
now she can't stand up
cos she's a triple cup
but her affliction
fits her job description.
Talking of wages
I been owed ages
from the corner shop
where we used to pop
pills and wine tasted
we were well wasted
battered and basted
then we'd mob the pub
then a city club
to rub-a-dub-dub
up against a Kirsty
who is hot and thirsty.
Best of all parties
Stop the City marches
bang outside my work,
see me go berserk
door wide open
latest slogan

windows broken
end up in a fight
in a cell all night
an my purse was light,
but I wasn't hindered
always been light-fingered,
boss got heavy-handed
challenged me red-handed
spent a fortnight stranded …
Then I moved to Southwark,
shacked up with a brother,
missus is my lover
rents a shop for cover,
only say I love her
so I get the sex free
but the blonde suspects me,
every day she texts me
says she wants my baby
and her name is Hayley.
Ello ello ello
here comes the ho
to get the cash I owe,
but *I'm* the gigolo
and *you've* got the dough
which means a battle so
the mic is fighting fit
to hear you spit some shit
on how I tricked your clit:
play the game, sister,
lay the blame, mister,
say the name, it's The …

# SHOOTER'S HILL

# Joined-up Writing
Memory Anesu Sergeant

1.

My son's a writer, aye, but he'll not write
to me, his poor old mam. I could be dead
these twenty years, sat in this chair, bone white.
Detective novels. *Crime pays, mam,* he said.
Only in books. In life, you pay twice over,
you cannot close a chapter, purge a sin.
I wronged my laddie, Ollie, Oliver.
Oliver Robson. Have you heard of him?

You've not? You're not from Tyneside are you, pet?
Milk, two sugars, boil the kettle, mind!
Ollie wrote seven books for Coronet,
his last one's autographed, see here, it's signed
*Oliver Robson.* Every paragraph
pure gold, a fortune in that autograph.

2.

She read her fortune in his autograph,
that Constance, but he'd not believe it, Ollie.
He got a grand advance for *Epitaph*
and bought this foisty townhouse to console me
after he married her, out of the blue.
Wouldn't let me arrange it, his own mother,
church wedding and all. He said 'I do'
knowing I disapproved. How could he love *her*?

She wasn't bonny, always overdressed,
I'd never understand her when she spoke.
Not that I'm prejudiced, some of my best
friends are foreign. These days folk are folk
but then was different: Constance was coloured, brown,
a name so long you'd sweat to break it down.

3.

Didn't belong, nigh verging on a breakdown,
and Ollie such a softy. African.
She'd not talk much, her face a constant frown,
must have been pity made him take her hand –
raped, or so she said. We were dead close,
Ollie and me, until she came, from nowhere:
whole house smelt of sadza; all his clothes
designer labels; cut his bonny hair

and marched him off to church twice on a Sunday!
Ollie, the atheist, who had no shame.
She must have used Black Magic that dark day
to make him say *I do* and sign his name.
We all lived here, I had no choice, she'd won.
Aye, Constance gained, and me, I lost my son.

4.

That year, she gained three stone, gave birth: a son.
Maurice: the image of his da, abroad
plugging his latest book, but back home soon.
Only said three words, Constance: *Praise the Lord.*
The flowers arrived first. Chrysanthemums,
delphiniums. I treated them as mine,
pretended that his note had said, *To Mam,*
and saw her eyes well up, dark as the Tyne.

Next day, that slim blue envelope, first post.
I steamed it open, read his spiky hand:
*My darling wife, Bless you! Now I'm the most
happy soul alive since God made man ...*
To see it written down, his love, his faith,
stabbed by his pen, I felt. Stabbed in the face.

5.

A stabbing pain the left side of my face,
I took a fresh white sheet and scrawled the line:
*Dear Constance, Whore of Babylon, unchaste,*
*you lied about the rape, the child's not mine ...*
I knew his hand, his long flamboyant 'I',
the exact angle, leaning to the right,
the mild slope of his 's', his loopless 'y'.
How could I not? I taught my son to write

his name when he was four. I trained his hand
to copy mine, letters with tiny tails
dying to be joined up – *You must leave England*
*and take your bastard with you* – cut his nails
to help his grip. Raised him for literature.
That fateful day I signed *his* signature.

6.


She fainted when she saw his signature ...
I helped her pack her suitcase, paid the fare –
it cost a fortune, flight to Africa.
I would have topped myself. What saved her? Prayer.
Poured myself a Scotch, if truth be telt,
when I got back, sat in this armchair, pet,
the chair she fed the laddie in that smelt
of milk and sadza. I still smell it yet.

I let it ring when Ollie phoned that night,
headache so bad, I couldn't take to bed.
He rang to say he'd just got off his flight –
each ring was like a stab wound in my head.
I heard the key, stood up, I don't know how.
If there's a God, I thought, God help me now!

7.

There is no God. Only you home helps now
who make weak tea and ask about my son.
There's dust on the computer screen. God knows,
I'm fast forgetting how to switch it on.
It hurts my hands to use a mobile phone,
he'll never ring it anyway, no doubt,
they'll not have phones in Africa. Alone,
I'm dying a slow death since he walked out.

I trawl the bookshops searching for his name,
gold embossed letters lighting up a spine,
five hundred pages full of guilt and shame.
But naught in there comes equal to my crime:
I signed his name; betrayed, in black and white,
my son, the writer. No, pet, he'll not write.

# DARTFORD

DARTFORD

# What Do Women Like Bes'?

Mrs Alice Ebi Bafa

My name is Mrs Alice Ebi Bafa,
I come from Nigeria.
I'm very fine, isn't it?
My nex' birthday I'll be … twenty-nine.
I'm business woman.
Would you like to buy some cloth?
I've all de latest styles from Lagos,
Italian shoe an' handbag to match,
lace, linen an' Dutch wax.
I only buy de bes'
an' I travel first class.

　　Some say I have blood on my han's
'cause I like to paint my nails red
but others call me femme fatale.
My father had four wives
so I've had five husband.
I cast a spell with my gap-tooth smile
an' my bottom power!
Three were good and two were bad.

　　The first three were old and rich
an' I was young and fit.
They died of exhaustion!
The first from Ghana, second Sierra Leone,
the third was white Englishman.
Short or tall, black or white,
I had race relations with dem.
They were quiet simple men
so I told lie to pepper de marriage.

*Why you drink Guinness in my neighbour's house-o?*
*Is she so fine in her Jimmy Shoe?*
*You go vex if I meet Justice Bafa*
*in Lagos bar and off my phone! Ah-ah!*
*Am I Delilah to cut off your head?*
I accused them of fornication
when they could barely stand on their two legs.
To enter my good book, they go beg!
    The fourth one was ladies' man,
I could not count his women on one han'
but he'd rage if I looked at another man.
He puff his ches' like King Solomon
with wife and concubine
but woman must be faithful and sober.
Such talk is not worth one kobo!
I am not a feminax,
I do not believe women are equal to men,
women are better!
Our chamber of Venus
is for both birth and pleasure.
I was very wild when I was young.
They called me Miss Highlife,
I was not considered a good wife
but I always respected my husban'.
He died when I returned from dis London.

The fifth one I married for love.
Chief Justice 'Aboniki' Bafa.
He was studying law at University of Ibadon.
He was not yet twenty-one,
wicked in bed and so handsome
but he liked pornographic magazine.
His favourite was *Playboy*.
One day I threw it on fire
to teach him a lesson.
He turned into wife batterer.
He was to regret his action.
I beat him till he begged for his ancestors!
Now we get on like house on fire.

Some say I'm a witchcraft
'cause I did not bear dem children.
They do not understand the Western medicine.
Since my first husban', from Ghana,
I had freedom of procreation.
He wanted ten children to pass my hip
but I learnt how to wield de whip.
Ghana is very advanced,
the female owns the children not de male.
This is their folktale
I tell in my own tongue:
'What Do Women Most Desire?'

A big man soldier
resided in king's household.
But outside de compound
he saw small girl, fourteen years of age
and took her by force!
He was disgraced and sentenced to death!
They must cut off his ... head.
In Ghana, woman was goddess.
But the queen pitied his sorrow,
she would spare his life
if he could answer question
*What thing is it that women most desire?*
in a year and tomorrow.

The soldier went on his two legs.
What do women like bes'?
Some said gold coin, or fine cloth,
some said man be chilli-pepper hot,
some said freedom, some said marriage,
some said we want husband think
we can keep secret to chest.
None were correct
and he failed the brain to guess.

The year end he mus' return.
Off road he heard beating of drum
an' saw plenty women, fit and young,
dancing in kente cloth,
traditional dress of Ghana.
They must give him answer.
But they disappeared into hot air.
Only an old old madame
suffering from eyes, leg rough like yam.

*Greetings, Nana! I beg you your wisdom.*
*What is the greatest desire of women?*
She smiled, *I reveal secret!*
*But sozaboy, promise*
*to grant my bes' wish.*
He gives her his word.
The old madame is elated.

   Nex' day old and young congregated
to hear soldier response.
Even mosquito quiet for his reply:
*Women desire to have sovereignty*
*over their husbands, or lovers.*
*They want to have mastery over him.*
*If I lie, I forfeit my head for sin.*
The palace sings jubilation.
No woman can contradict him,
wife, widow or virgin.
But the old madame with eyes
must have her wish:
That he must take her hand in marriage!
He think say it worse than death
but soldier mus' honour his debt.

   That night old madame be smiling in bed.
It pain him to look his newlywed.
*Husban', pay your dues to wife!*
*Am I too poor for love?*
*I can amen' myself, Sir,*
*but you must amen' yourself also.*
*Your family not give virtue, dat from God.*
*Your pride not worth one cedi!*
*You say I old. Respect your elder!*

*And if I ugly, I not take lover.*
*Ugliness an' age keep me chaste.*
Still he refuse to look her face.
*I make amen', my husban'. Choose!*
*I remain ugly an' old*
*an' faithful to your body,*
*or young an' fine and flirt any body …*
What a dilemma!
He frown till he resemble old papa.
*My wife,* he says, *Choose for your husband.*
*I place myself in your capable hands.*

This so pleases the old old madame.
*Kiss me, my husban', so handsome!*
*You have given me power you should.*
*I shall be both beautiful an' good.*
*Look my face when cock crow,*
*I am very pleasing to you.*
Her prophecy came to pass
and the marriage consummated in bliss …

So she married a rapist
but he learnt his lesson.
May God give us young submissive husband!

You like my headtie?
It's de latest fashion.
They sell like hot cake on Victoria Island.
Fifty pounds.
I give you discount 'cause I like your smile.
The quality is very good.
If I take off more I will not make profit
an' I travel to Lagos nex' week.
Make it my lucky day.
Please, I beg you!

# The Devil in Cardiff
Huw Fryer Jones

D'ya hear Robbo got sent down again?
When a snitch gets sent down
what chance for the rest of us, eh?
Allowed one call and he calls me,
the div. I ses, *Where are ya?* He ses,
*Hell! No signal down 'ere. Can't bloody text!*
I ses, *What you doing down there, moron?*
   Ses he met a man in the Dragon,
asks him what he does and Robbo
ses he's a bailiff, helluva sly, Robbo.
Man ses he's a bailiff too, for his sins,
an' Robbo gets the bevvies in.
Talk breaking, entering, weapons,
summonses, like, repossessions.
Sell his nain for a pint, Robbo.
Pint of bitter for me … Robbery
but he got a suspended … So they're playing pool
an' man says he's not a bailiff at all
he's the Devil Incarnate!
Robbo ses, *I was the devil in Cardiff*
*meself last weekend. Broke the ASBO,*
*banned from South Wales, me … Robbo,*
*Robert Owen.* They shake hands like
they're arm wrestling an' Robbo winks.
Ses he's got a job on the side selling
dope to the cops, raking it in.
Thick as thieves, they were. Ta!

Closing time, there's a lad in a Lada,
won't start. He's revving it hoarse,
cursing it to hell. Freezing cold, it was.
Car's choking like an old bag
then comes back to life. *Thank God*, ses the lad,
drives off. Robbo laughs, *If you're the Devil
you shoulda taken the car, you div*,
but the Devil ses no, he only takes what's his
when the curse means business,
none of your half-baked.
Robbo ses he'll teach him the tricks of the trade.

They're well out of town now
an' Robbo stops at this bungalow,
peeling paint, leaky roof,
knocks on the door with his leather glove
and this old dear opens up, *Oh, it's you!*
tries to slam the door but he pushes through.
She says, *I owe nothing, I'm a poor, old woman.*
But Robbo's got this fake summons –
non-payment of a fine with interest.
*Pay up or pay the price*, he ses,
and the Devil's laughing in his overcoat
like he just told an old joke.
Nothing on the shelf but a teapot
full of old coins. Robbo grabs it,
empties the coins on the carpet.
*Mine*, he says, *To cover an old debt
I paid for you, on a street corner.*
Helluva sly, Robbo. She says, *You're
wicked, Robert Owen, I only*

*knew one man, my late husband, Dai,*
then starts speaking Welsh, like. *Repent*
*or the Devil take your soul and the teapot ancient!*
Robbo tells her where she can put
her repentance and the Devil bags him and the teapot
non-stop to Hell! Dying for a pint, he is.
Only serve tea down there, and bloody biscuits …
Bitter for me … He'll be back here
in less than a month, though, bet you a fiver,
they'll be beggin' him to go.
Get an ASBO from Hell, Robbo.

# Arse Dramatica
Geoff Sumner

Door-to-door salesmen? Scum!
I should know, use ta be one.
Me an' this geezer John worked North London

where the Newtons is. Pensioners in semis,
read the *Guardian*, give to charities,
know the type? We was the bees knees

in bullshit. Gift of the gob.
Commission-only and we made a few bob
on the stain-free carpet job

but wasn't enough. John had a plan.
Fake insurance, our first scam.
Made a few grand.

Then, NADA, for dumb people
who can't act. John turned on the babble,
quote the Bible

from Eve to the ark
if it helped with the big ask.
Straight from the devil's arse!

I leave him to it, go down the boozer.
He looks up Thomas, old geezer,
bedridden, East End miser,

41

cash-wadded mattress,
made masses,
John 'knows' the missus:

*Morning gorgeous. How's the old man?*
She winks, *Bent as a white van.*
An' John says, all deadpan,

*Collecting for me charity, NADA.*
*National Academy for Dumb Actors.*
*Thomas, be our benefactor!*

Sits on the end of the bed,
missus brings sliced meat, sliced bread,
Thomas shakes his head:

*Fuck off!*
*I've given a grand to you and your 'staff'.*
*Enough's enough!*

I'd scarper. Not John.
Knows how to turn it on
an' the wife crosses her bacons.

*Sounds like a good cause, luv!*
Every line you could think of,
John pulls it off:

how they got to build new offices,
how it's giving jobs to the jobless.
Load of old cobblers.

*If you got no charity, Thomas, know what?*
*You're nothing. Nada. Diddly Squat.*
*Now show us what ya got!*

Plonks the form on the eiderdown,
*Have a butcher's at this. Come on,*
*sign your name in neon!*

Thomas smiles, *Alright, I'm smitten*
*but you know I don't do nothin' written.*
*Got somethin' better I keep hidden.*

He gestures to the cover, *Put your arm*
*behind me*, an' John's groping round his arse,
hoping for a windfall 'for the arts'

when Thomas farts! Loud as a carthorse,
*Share that with your workforce!*
And John's a whippet off a racecourse,

you won't believe the stench!
Now he's sitting on the pub bench
plotting revenge

while the whole pub's trying to decide
how John'll equally divide
that blast from the backside!

To this day, John's pissed off
but you can't argue with the pay-off.
He had it coming. End of.

# STONE

# I Go Back to May 1967
Yejide Idowu-Clarke

*After Sharon Olds*

I see them standing outside their family compounds.
I see my father wearing a white agbadan and
crocodile shoes, instructing his driver by the
spiked iron gate of their complex, he is just
twenty-four but already a big man in Lagos. It is
rainy season, the air heavy with his looming proposal. I
see my mother walking barefoot on the red dust road to her
village, a calabash on her head, wearing her only cloth and
crucifix, she has just fetched water from the well.
They have not yet met, today they will be married.
My father will arrive in his Cadillac to
translate her into his bride, adorned with gold.
I want to approach them and say Stop,
I am begging you—you are not a bad woman,
he is not a good man, he is going to put you on trial
like Job: you will bear him a daughter, and later a son,
and each time he will say his people have turned against you
because you are from a small village and not educated,
each baby must be removed by force from your breast
(but he will secretly place us in care of my aunt
to attend the best schools in the country)
and you will draw the sign of the cross on our heads,
your womb will cry out but you will not disgrace him
for you promised to honour and obey; in time, he will claim
he wants a new wife, believes in one man one wife
and wants a divorce, will send you back to your village

barefoot and bareheaded with barely a cloth to cover
the belly that bore him two children; then order you back
like a housegirl to manage the house and the wedding feast
for his beautiful new wife from a good family
who resembles you, because it is I, your daughter,
standing before you, young, adorned with gold;
and only when you say, *Oga, please I beg you,*
*do not treat your new wife the way you have treated me,*
will he reveal his deception to test your faith
in him and your love of the Lord Jesus Christ. I want to
approach them, there in the late May heat and say it,
her hungry pretty face turning towards me
slow motion with the weight of the calabash,
his arrogant handsome face turning towards me
slowly with the precious weight on his mind.
But I do not say it. I want to live my life. I
take them up like Shango and Oshun
mahogany dolls and rub them together
at the hips, wood on wood, as if to
make fire from them, and I say
Do what is God's will and I will bear witness.

# That Beatin' Rhythm
Soul Merchant

Once Upon a Time, in the Land Of 1000 Dances, January married May. What is This Thing Called Love? Some say, Love Is a Serious Business; some say, Love Is a Trap. He's The Bachelor, She's Not The Marrying Kind. He's Mr Big Shot *Got My Mind Made Up* and she's a Country Girl *Talkin' 'Bout Poor Folks, Thinkin' 'Bout My Folks*. He says *I've Struck It Rich* but some say *she* Cashing In. He's Too Old for her and yet, they (Just Like) Romeo and Juliet. Adam and Eve.

And I'm Damien, Agent 00 Soul from the Backstreet, the Image Of a Man. Saw a Job Opening for a Mr Clean to Lend a Hand to Little Old Man, January. He bought the House For Sale, The House Next Door, huge as a Haunted Castle. I fell The Big Oak Tree to make furniture an' sing The Work Song as I'm clearing Bricks, Broken Bottles and Sticks outside. There's a Storm Warning and I Run for Cover from the Spring Rain, the first Time I see May, the Lady In Green. She's a Flower Child, a Wild One. I say *Stop Girl*, but she Keep On Walking, Surrounded By a Ray Of Sunshine. Am I Cold, Am I Hot. I Got the Fever. I Love Her So Much (It Hurts Me).

January puts the Band Of Gold on her Third Finger Left Hand an' they Sign On the Dotted Line. Then we Dearly Beloved Come Back to bass. Ain't Nothin' But a Houseparty. There be Soul Food: Sliced Tomatoes and Green Onions. There be Apples, Peaches, Pumpkin Pie. There be Street Talk, Sweet Talk and Melodies.

—*There Was a Time*, says January, *when I'd Philly Dog Around the World but I'm Tired Of Running Around. Since I Found My Baby, Home Is Where the Heart Is. When you're old as The Big Oak Tree, Make Sure (You Have Someone Who Loves You), a Little Young Lover or Time Will Pass You By. Some say Ain't No Soul Left In These Old Shoes but I'm forever a Night Owl. I'm Com'un Home In the Morning. Pity My Feet.*

January, you Keep On Talking, I've Got My Eyes On You, Blushing Bride. Ain't laying my Cards On the Table but My Heart Is Calling. Music, The Beat, That Beatin' Rhythm. January leads May Out On the Floor and it's Getting Mighty Crowded. I Can't Be Still, gotta Dance, Dance, Dance: The Horse, The Boston Monkey, The Cool Jerk. I'm Where It's At, Look At Me, Look At Me, girl, What's My Chances? When they left, I Just Kept On Dancing but my Shoes got the Cold-Hearted Blues.

Love Love Love, I be Love Sick. Heart Trouble but Nobody Knows What's Going On In My Mind But Me. This Love-Starved Heart (Is Killing Me). I S.O.S. so she know Something's Wrong. Here She Comes, my Black-Eyed Girl, to Help Me.

—*Only Your Love Can Save Me*, I whisper. *Call Me, Call Me Tomorrow!*

—*I Must Love You*, she smiles, *I Dream Of You. But January's a Jealous Lover. Keeps a Shotgun.*

—*Don't Worry 'Bout Me. I Can Take Care Of Myself, but Gotta Have Your Love, Can't Wait No Longer, It's Torture.*

We plan to find some Love Time. She'll Joe Tex me. It's our Deep Dark Secret.

Then, All Of a Sudden, January's struck blind as Ray Charles. Be's That Way Sometimes. A Blessing In Disguise, If You Ask Me. They call Dr Love but January says to May,

—*I Don't Need No Doctor. I Need You! Don't Pity Me.*

Mister Misery for weeks, sees nothing but Ten Shades Of Blue. Only Sweet Soul Music make him Keep On Keeping On. He'd die for Suspicion.

—*They're Talkin' About Me. They say You Don't Love Me Anymore. Tell Me It's Just a Rumour, Baby.*

—*Why Picture Me Gone? Baby Can't You See, I'll Always Love You.*

Before he'd never Let Her Go Out Of Sight, now she Serving a Sentence of Life in a Prison of Love. He says,

—*Baby Let Me Hold Your Hand. Never Gonna Let You Go. What Good Am I Without You?*

How can I Love My Baby now she Never Alone? Calls for a Whole New Plan. Got To Find a Way.

January got a Top Secret room, he call 'My Garden Of Eden' where they Do It. Vinyl Heaven In the Afternoon, Wall To Wall Heartaches. Raised stage made from The Big Oak Tree, decks, A Lot Of Loving Goin' Round the turntable. Nobody Knows where it's at, Nobody But Me. She cut me a Key To My Happiness from the Master Key so we can get A Little Togetherness.

And today Sweeter Than the Day Before cos January says,

—*Let's Go To That Lovin' Place,*

an' May Joe Tex me. I Run Like the Devil to that One Room Paradise and Up Jump the Devil on stage like I Playing Hide and Seek. No steps to climb Step By Step. I'm Waiting for you, Lady In Green, to open the Green Door, an' I'll Open the Door To Your Heart.

They Walk On In. January Just Can't Trust Nobody since he blind. Thinks She Got Another Man.

—*May, Do You Love Me or are you Somebody Else's Sweetheart?*

—*What Kind Of Lady you think I am? I'm a Good Woman, Still True To You and I Keep the Faith. What More Do You Want?*

—*Little Darlin', I'm So So Sorry. What Can I Do Just To Prove I Love You?* An' May says,

—*I Feel an Urge Coming On for That Beatin' Rhythm. Gotta find The Right Track for Our Love. I'm Not Strong Enough to Get On Up onto the stage, it's Ten Miles High. If You Love Me, Get On Your Knees so I can climb Up and Over to the decks.*

—*For You Baby, I'll Do Anything.*

Some say, Love Ain't Nothin' (But a Monkey On Your Back) an' that monkey Keep On Climbing up to where I'm Standing. She play 'I Really Love You' real loud. We gotta Take a Chance, Time's a-Wasting. Temptation Is Calling My Name, Girl, Don't Make Me Wait. She's Turning My Heartbeat Up, Oh My Darling! No Time for Interplay, I'm The Snake In Paradise, Oh, Yeah, Yeah, Yeah …

And Suddenly January yells,

—*What? Oh No Not My Baby! I Can See Him Loving You!!!*

No Fortune Teller predict this. I'm In a World Of Trouble. And I think, Be Careful Girl, Better Use Your Head. Say It Isn't So and May says,

—*Sweetheart Darling, a Last-Minute Miracle! I'm So Glad your sight's Come Back. Baby Can't You See, Damien's teaching me the Love Hustle? Don't deny me One Little Dance!*

—*Who Are You Trying To Fool? I Can See Him Making Love To You, Baby!* But May says,

*—You're Barkin' Up the Wrong Tree. I love oldies not newies. I want a Big Bad Wolf not a Baby Boy. You Too Darn Soulful, That's Why I Love You.* And January says,

*—If I Could Only Be Sure. I Was Blind, maybe Something's Wrong With These Eyes. Just a Little Misunderstanding. If You've Been Cheatin', I Don't Like It (But I Love You). I'll Forgive and Forget. May, We Were Made For Each Other, Like Adam and Eve. Do I Love You (Indeed I Do).*

Now we Right Back Where We Started From. It's Torture listening to A Lover's Concerto, Standing In the Shadows Of Love. Give me The Real Thing. I'm Hung Up On Your Love, May, He'll Never Love You Like I Do. I'm Stepping Out of the Picture, I'm On My Way, I'm Gone. But I'll Never Forget You. My Heart Is Calling You Baby. Every Beat Of My Heart.

# GRAVESEND

# Fine Lines
Jeu'di Squires

You
knew
blue
    was my colour   the blue-black
        of an old tattoo   you drew
           blood        with your sword-pen-gun
             I want you
back

   No one-night-stud
     on a shire horse
        seeking princess in chintz dress   you were the

Fire Horse
   wild steed I rode bareback
held your hair for reins as you bolted like a stud
   each strange steel stud
     on your right ear gleaming in the true-black

*Don't touch my metal,* you spat
   so I held back
     from your rook   tragus   lobe
       three steel globes
     though my tongue longed to lick
     those flickering glittering ellipses …

No striptease
    baring of the soul      you were
        pierced thick as chainmail
            metal where you should have had a heart
    I couldn't read the body art
        infiltrate the ink of each tattoo
            mine a fine line      get
through
to
you


Your body spread out like the map
  of a falcon in full-feathered-flight
      wanting to be unicorn
one breath on your rook and you bucked
      your tragus and you flew
    I rode you halfway round the globe till I was saddle-sore
and never coming back


You scratched an outline   on my bare back
  your sword-pen-gun
      blacked ink in my skin   deep as melanin
you carved my back a gold frame
  ornate with leaves
    but left before you filled in the picture

so my back became the mirror mirror
        on the shelf
you looked into its glass and saw yourself
in the future        leaving
    now I'm sitting here rekindling your memory
like an old flame

You backstabbed
    but I healed        scabbed
        like an oil painting
now I'm reflecting
    on this old gold ring
        you left on my finger   the day you left

With this ring
    I opened your mind a book and read
            in fine gold letters
            *Don't touch my metal*
déjà vu   but the urge was too strong
    I put my tongue to your lobe
        and you bolted
            leaving me        singed   the wild bird
who
flew
too
    close to your fire and scorched her wings

59

Betrothed   to a future   perfect   you
  I read the minds of gold-studded unicorns
    with fake horns       who
      see their fate framed in the fading blue-
    black of my back

    when I turn my back
      on them
      for not being you

# Makar
Frankie Lynn

*If you have built castles in the air, your work need not be lost; that is where
they should be. Now put the foundations under them.*

— Henry David Thoreau

To Denmark's Freetown Christiania
my mind transports me when it's overcast,
when there's a thunderstorm or night draws near
I close my eyes: the heady hit of grass
from hash stalls; houses honed from wood and glass,
one flaking door, its mirrored hall, the spiral
staircase: on that battered sofa – Arild,

his purple dreads engrossed in his own story,
Arild, who flew too close to gold, dropped out
and landed here, the tumble-down, three-storey
Sesame House, home of the down, the out,
who come to learn how to survive without:
to make do, make things, make things up, to dare
to fabricate a castle out of air

under a master, aka The Artist,
whose learned thoughts flow deeper than a fjord
and made of Arild's mind a palimpsest
on which he wrote three notes that formed a chord
till Arild knew the world within a word
and one long night, through spelling out a spell,
cobbled a cabin made of cockle shells

with seven caves, each cave singing the sea
and when the sun came up his cabin shone,
everyone marvelled at his sorcery;
but Freetown states you can't create a home
without consent: a clash, and Arild's gone,
squeezed out, forced out, pushed out down Pusher Street ...
now here we meet him, crossing Princes Street,

Edinburgh: now an actor, single, shaved,
who slept on someone's floor two years ago
till luck ran out; homeless: then one night caved
a home inside the Mound, its walls aglow
with books, books, books, except for one framed photo
where you'd expect a mirror: Hogmanay,
Deirdre and Angus on their wedding day,

his dearest friends: Angus, bleached blond, well-built;
Deirdre, brunette, petite; she made his outfit –
bubblewrap jacket, seersucker kilt
to match her jeans bejewelled with pomegranate
seeds, her bubble shoes the perfect fit:
made for each other – Deirdre wears the trousers,
Angus, the kilt – they're solid, safe as houses

till late midsummer's eve, Angus away
in England for a month, everyone high
on homebrew except Arild who today
must spell it out, confess to Deirdre why
it's agony to look her in the eye
for every time he looks at her, he's cursed,
must say those words a thousand times rehearsed:

*I must make love to you.* Two years he's made
light of it, nothing of it, forged, invented
a virtue of necessity, betrayed
nothing, but love, drunk on itself, unwanted,
made a pass, yet Deirdre's strong, undaunted:
*I will,* she laughs, *if, for three weeks, my Danish
bookworm, you can make the Castle vanish;*

not knowing at that instant Arild texts
The Artist in his hammock out in Freetown
who knows, this master artist-architect,
both how to build things up and pull things down;
how the right words, verb, adjective and noun,
in the right order, uttered in the air
can turn a sandstone castle to thin air

for the small sum of a thousand euros
which isn't much when love feels more like death
so Arild learns the craft and each day grows
as well versed as the witches in Macbeth
predicting destiny with sound and breath,
till August brings the Festival: day one,
Edinburgh wakes to find her Castle gone!

Tourists, their eyes set on wide-angle lens:
actors drop fliers, workers, shoppers dazed;
Angus and Deirdre coming back from friends
stare at the huge blank empty space, amazed
that overnight, history's been erased.
Throwaway sentence uttered on the solstice,
Deirdre chokes, remembering her promise.

*I gave my* word *to Arild,* she tells Angus
who pales and holds her hand to keep from shaking,
The Royal Mile indifferent to their anguish.
There's no way out but take the road not taken –
if Arild knows the art of dark unmaking
what more can he unleash, unearth, undo:
*Make love to him, but let your heart be true.*

A stone's throw from the Castle to the Mound,
each painful step as heavy as a stone
and each stone building weighted to the ground,
each cobbled wynd is whispering *Run home!*
A kiss, she takes the final steps alone,
her mind reverting to their wedding day,
that photograph. But now her lips are grey.

Arild, who caved a home inside the Mound,
is squatting deep inside its entrance, Arild,
who sees in Deirdre's bearing how profound
true love can be; his monumental oral
feat has spelled out love's double-headed arrow:
physical, headstrong, passionately selfish,
psychical, heartfelt, passionately selfless.

*You're both too good for me. Go back to him.*
Arild is spent and yet he owes The Artist,
who, hearing of his pupil's altruism,
cancels the debt. Now Arild knows that art is
the making of him: art is his catharsis,
through words, words, words, he'll purge the pain, the doubt.
The cave erupts and pushes Arild out

to reinvent himself again, a makar:
to make a poem; hone it, room by room,
stanza by stanza; form, on one blank acre
from bricks and mortar, breath and metre, home;
to mount the spiral staircase of his poem,
take a battered volume off the shelf,
open a random page, and read himself ...

# STROOD

# Reconstruction

Kiranjeet Singh

*The 'honour killer', Gino De Luca, has today been convicted of manslaughter of his teenage daughter. Photographer De Luca, 44, was suffering from severe depression at the time of the killing. He beheaded his daughter, Virginia, 14, then delivered her severed head to alleged blackmailer, Tony 'The Ape' Ferarro, 37. Ferraro faces allegations of child abuse. De Luca will serve his 8-year sentence at a secure psychiatric hospital.*

**– *The Echo*, 20 June, 1984.**

Had her dad's red hair but wild as if [1]
ragged it. He snapped; she knew
how broke his lens was, gave what
it wanted, a game of he ...
But *he* became real. My Gino did
some shots for that man, Ferarro: had to.
He, The Ape, Warholed his flat with young
redheads, would call them his 'girls'.
Had her headshot; wanted to have her. He
dealt in photos, lies, told Gino she had
no De Luca blood, found his Achilles with that.
My man lost it. Not his baby ...
Not the man I married in this photo
snapped on his way to court, and
the headline, MANSLAUGHTER, the
thrust of it. My Gino only
said one word, *Sorry*, that was his way,
to leave it hanging cold. He had to.
I couldn't face him, or the knife. I save
the papers where I still see Virginia ...
They said each time Gino faced the mirror, it was
her pale face his eyes belonged to ...

# Profit

Yves Depardon

*Radix malorum est Cupiditas. Ad Thimotheum, 6°.*

*Ladies and Gents and Miscellaneous,*
is how I start my Feel-Good talks, *Tonight*
*my lecture is on Greed, yes, Avarice,*
*the deadliest of sins. I stand before you,*
*guru of Gordon Gekko, 'Greed is Good',*
*a liar, forger, thief: thigh-deep in sin.*
*Oh yes, I've had my innings and my outings –*
*more than once, I've peaked, top of the hit list*
*and lived. I'm vicious, too wicked to die.*
*You want to know the consequence of sinning?*
*Don't ask a saint, O ladies, ask a sinner.*
And then I cast my eye upon the crowd,
nodding my head as if remembering
a heinous deed for which I paid twice over.
And after this dramatic pause, my punchline:
*Radix malorum est Cupiditas.*
A pinch of Latin to add gravitas:
*Love of money is the root of evil.*
Already, some are squirming in their seats
and one or two are weeping. I take pains
to look the part, my greying hair dyed yellow,
stringier than Stringfellow, greasy
and shoulder length. I dress androgynous,
a velvet robe, touch of the Vatican
but don't mention the G word or the J word.
As for my voice, I camp it up an octave,

70

to freak old ladies out, and thrill the queens,
address my business partner as 'my *partner*'
and roll my eyes a lot. They love the act.
*You see this volume here?* I hold it up,
You Wouldn't Want to Go There: A Confession,
*my life, my death in print. Read it to learn*
*how NOT to go to Heaven. Me, in hardback.*
*You won't see me outside the pearly gates,*
*I'm going somewhere hot by Business Class —*
*Radix malorum est Cupiditas.*
*It's hot, hot-off-the-press, singed by the fires*
*of Hell, self-help with bells on. See this water?*
*Cloudy as a Welsh weekend, it's blessed*
*with healing properties, the minerals*
*will cure all ills from asthma to depression.*
*Who'd like a sip? Take care, it's medicine,*
*not Evian. You may be wondering*
*why I wear a diamanté wristband?*
*Crims Against Crime. Follow us on Facebook.*
*For a small sum, you too could raise awareness …*
They lap it up: the dogdy rainwater
in bottles, and the sparkly rubber bands,
they've come to spend spend spend. When they've suspended
all disbelief, I raise my crystal glass:
*Radix malorum est Cupiditas.*
*And then I roll my eyes:* 'What shall it profit
a man, if he shall gain the whole wide world, and
lose his own soul?' *Mark 8, verse 36.*
*Ladies and Gentlemen, I lost my soul!*
It's then I pause to drink the glass of claret
and eat some dry white bread. You want a story?

71

This is the tale I tell them: I grew up
somewhere not in London nor in Kent –
believe you me, you wouldn't want to go there.
I formed a gang, we swore blood brotherhood,
shared the same scar, called ourselves The Lifers.
Just three of us, the twisted twins and me.
Handbags at first but then we graduated
to break-ins, made a thousand pounds a week,
not to mention all the benefits
under false identities. We spent it
on wine, women, William, as in Hill.
Oh, I could tell you, on St George's Night
how we paid homage to the red, the white!
And how we swore allegiance, how we swore
'Fuck this, screw you!' until the air was blue
with uniforms, the rest of it's a blur,
but time is cash ... One night, the twins and I
were in the local wine bar, when we heard
that Baz, a virgin member we were grooming
had been done over fatal by the rival
gang, The Deathwish, led by Death. We were
tooled up, our hand-cut suits lined thick with knives
and bored as hell. I smashed our empty bottle
of red against the bar, '*Death, thou shalt die!*'
and off we sped. We found this ancient geezer,
smelling of piss, face like a fist. I kicked him,
felled him like a deck of cards. 'Fuck you!
Ain't you lived long enough? Drop dead, you bastard!'
He turned his head to face me, 'Go on, kill me!
I'm fucked, nothing but flesh and blood and skin.
At Death's door. Death, you wanker, let me in!'

'Where's Death?' I kick again, 'Death,' croaked the tramp,
'condemned block. Number 4.' And there we found him,
not Death, but something far more entertaining:
the suitcase, crammed with filthy dirty lucre.
Someone's gold, someone who didn't make it,
so hot it hurt our eyes to look at it.
'Brothers,' I cried, 'this calls for celebration.
Champagne's not good enough! Some Charlie Chaplin!'
And off I sped to get some choice white powder
from my associates, murderous arsenic.
You think I'd share my profit with those arselicks?
And back I sped to that dark place lit up
with *all that glisters*. There, the twins embraced me,
with grunts and grins and then the stranglehold
from one, and from the other, seven stab wounds!
They watched me bleed to death in that foul squat,
forming the arsenic into two fat lines
and me, I watched them snort like no tomorrow
and twist and writhe and die a young man's death
before I fell into a ten-year coma.
    *The wages of sin are death*. I flat-lined twice
and twice they called the priest. When I woke up,
the nurse looked shell-shocked, ancient, and addressed me
as Sir. I stretched my arms to yawn and noticed
my scar, raised, red. And then I spoke. My voice
raised like a preacher's, organ, bass and brass:
*Radix malorum est Cupiditas* ...
    If people want to read the uncut version,
it's in my book, *You Wouldn't Want to Go There*.
Sold out. I have a few deluxe editions
at thirty pounds, each one signed by the master

of motivation, M, who wrote the foreword,
and me. I take all credit, debit cards.
Of course you may be steeped in avarice,
too miserly to part with such a sum?
Perhaps a wristband, sir? You look like you're
in need of moral guidance. Go to hell?
Already been there, thank you. Water, madam?
You could drop dead tomorrow, there's no future,
only now. It's *your* life, make your choice.
Two for a fiver. Don't all rush at once.

# ROCHESTER

ROCHESTER

# Things
Klaudia Schippmann

*I don't need love*
*For what good will love do me?*
*Diamonds never lie to me*
*For when love's gone*
*They'll lustre on*
   – 'Diamonds are Forever', Don Black

My wedding ring? I never take
it off. I once made the mistake,
and paid for it. The money stopped.
I took the bus and window shopped,
seeing in the window's filth
the dull reflection of myself
till something caught my eye, a spark:
I stared stock-still till it grew dark –
a necklace with a ruby clasp,
if I could plunge my hand through glass …
Nothing else mattered. Hubby paid
to keep my name from the front page …
  My wedding ring. Its antique gold
understatement leaves me cold,
its clean cut vowels that say, I'm rich.
I much prefer the nouveau riche,
stone-encrusted blatant bling
that sparks from my engagement ring,
such sparkling wit – such repartee,
these diamonds winking back at me –
this emerald-cut centre stone

takes centre stage at each At Home.
Let bling deliver blah de blah
to save me from my next faux pas,
I have no time for metaphor:
I make my statement with Dior
and diamonds but, beneath these clothes,
I'm plain Octavia who loathes
Society. I prefer things
that catch the light, designer rings.

See this? I keep it in the shade,
I've never worn it. Custom-made.
It gleams so loud it might express
my secret to the gutter press
how once I blagged the total of
a thousand pounds to pay it off.
Both our joint accounts were closed
since hubby got me 'diagnosed'
and bloody jeweller wanted cash.
Ever since the credit crash
he's hounded me. That night I shone,
talked with my hands, I turned them on,
Octavia, the talking doll,
has learnt her lines, the protocol,
I flash these lovely diamonds at
The Money Monk. And he winks back.

I state my debt: he makes a bid.
I don't do small talk: he talks big.
Says he needs to check some data,
says he loves me two days later –
hubby's cousin, business partner,
Money Monk, renowned for barter,

says he only wants one thing
and covers up my wedding ring
with twenty notes all crisp and new:
*A thousand, for a night with you!*
I'd rather not become involved
but Money's spoken: problem solved.
I acquiesce and realise
the Monk has malachite for eyes ...

   Hubby's away, a business trip,
he left that morning. When I strip
for Monk, he says his body aches.
I love the sound his Rolex makes,
its subtle tick, as we embrace
I marvel at its jewelled face.
And when we're done, I call a cab
and pay the last instalment, cash.
Perfecto. Who needs money, love?
I prefer things, I always have.

   And that would be the end, had not
hubby returned and spoilt the plot
by asking for the, now defunct,
thousand pounds I got from Monk,
the thousand pounds I thought my own
The Money Monk procured on loan –
he borrowed it from *hubby*'s stash
but paid it back through *me*, in cash.

   I hate surprises, and my gut
response is blunt confession but
my therapist often asserts,
sometimes it's good to lie: truth hurts.
*I spent it.* Not untrue, I can't

quite lie but hubby's adamant,
eyes sparkling with anger. I
widen my lapis lazuli
and lip, through 'Dazzling Amethyst',
an offer that he can't resist:
to pay my debt to him in bed ...

    This ring, I keep deposited –
some things are better left unsaid.

# Sharps an Flats
Missy Eglantine

*Yet spak this child, whan spreynd was hooly water*
*And song* O Alma redemptoris mater!
                                        – Geoffrey Chaucer

Dear Mum,
              It's your son, J, chattin on a mix made
in Heaven, don't hit the fade switch b4 it's played:
remember, used 2 have perfect pitch but my pitch paid
a rich trade when I got cut off by a switchblade.
No need 2 pray, U ain't hearin voices, this score is
the same voice age 7, spoke like a thesaurus,
wrote long stories, opened my throat like the dawn chorus
in God's gang, my chords sang *Alma redemptoris.*

Mum, I woz singin *O Alma* when the blade blast,
tune makes broken windows rainbow like stained glass,
not lookin out 4 the snake in the grass
gets a boy slain in the vein by the caned class.
I took the short cut, a door shut, I woz deaf, blind
2 *Shut the f\*\*k up!* Yeah, I mucked up their dead line.
I woz *stuck up* and my throat woz a red line,
at 7, hit Heaven b4 I hit the headlines.

*Mater*? Made a martyr 4 backchattin in Latin
sharps an flats, I had no idea what I woz chattin.
2 boys from the back flats, thought I woz backstabbin
so they stabbed with a sharp, 2 cut me off from battlin
like a rich kid. So the switch did the talk, then the mans lied,
boys in blue twisted your words till U were hands-tied
in prayer, the nuns held U up like when dad died,
grief crashin down your face like a landslide.

Mum, smile, it's me, J, broader and far taller
than the boy whose voice broke before he could call for
help, the star scholar who grew far from squalor,
Do Re Mi Fa, with my spar, Damilola.
Got my chords cut but I'm singin like it's Sunday,
boys got shut up, an I know this, that one day
you'll come stay, so peace! Remember what the nuns say,
*Love conquers all.* I sign off,

Your loving son, J.

# Artful Doggerel:
## *Sir Topaz vs Da Elephant – Round 3*
Sir Topaz & Da Elephant

*... grime sounds as if it had been made for a boxing gym, one where the fighters have a lot of punching to do but not much room to move.*
                                                    – Sasha Frere-Jones

I be
    Sir Topaz, E3 bling king
    so dazzling you be blinking
    pack punches till they sink in
    I be Twitter, you be LinkedIn
    online the girls I reel in
    it's pep-talk that I deal in
    but Pepsi's not the real thing
    ask your homegirl how she feeling

(applause)


    *Da Elephant, I'm eloquent,*
    *the heavyweight of grime,*
    *me rhymes are sick, I'm gonna pick*
    *your pocket full of rhyme,*
    *South London's king, so I'm linked in,*
    *you're out to lunch on bhang,*
    *like David slew Goliath, you*
    *will slay yourself with slang*

(applause)

You be
    so slow you slump on the bassline
    I jump off the beat, don't waste time
    hundred kilos, watch your waistline,
    I tasted your girl, she taste fine
    I'm hungry, speaking of lunchtime
    I burn up cals on the frontline
    your trunk's defunct, her cunt's mine,
    you be out for 9 on that punchline

(mad applause and booing)

       *You double dealt below the belt*
       *but I will bust your screen,*
       *you shoot your load in virtual mode*
       *cos you're a fairy queen,*
       *you stole my girl, she said you smell*
       *your dick's a Bic, a biro,*
       *you write your rhymes and learn your lines*
       *and gamble all your giro*

(mad applause and booing)

You be
    breaking up in your nearly new style
    mess with me but you know it's futile
    I got your girl, she's nubile,
    you got three heads, look at you, vile,
    one says I'm gay but you retrial
    one says I shafted your female
    one says fuck-all cos it's penile!
    Stick that up your trunk for a freestyle!

(mad applause)

    *You got no creds, I got three heads,*
    *they're body, mind and soul*
    *but dickhead, you have only one*
    *that's why you're on the dole*

(applause)

I be
    Sir Topaz, claiming my last dole
    just signed a deal in charcoal
    not a fat cat sitting on me arsehole,
    shoot rhymes from a metaphor arsenal,
    one step ahead, metatarsal,
    up there with Wiley & Rascal,
    you be doggerel, I'm artful,
    Elephant, fuck off back to your Castle …

(mad applause …)

# Unfinished Business
Mel O'Brien

*Conveniently, cowardice and forgiveness look identical at a certain distance.*
*Time steals your nerve.*

– 'Memento Mori', Jonathan Nolan

That night, it rained so hard
it was biblical. The Thames sunk the promenade,
spewing up so much low life.
It's a week since they beat up my wife,
put five holes in my daughter. I know who they are.
I know why. I'm three shots away from the parked car
in a blacked-out car park. My wife cries,
*Revenge too sweet attracts flies.*
Even blushed with bruises she looks good. She's lying
on the bed, next to me. *Honey, I'm fine.*
Tonight I caught her, hands clasped, kneeling,
still from a crime scene.
I didn't bring my wife to Gravesend for this.
What stops me, cowardice?
None of them, even Joe, has the right to live.
How can I forgive?

How can I forgive
none of them? Even Joe has the right to live.
What stops me? Cowardice.
I didn't bring my wife to Gravesend for this
still from a crime scene.
Tonight I caught her, hands clasped, kneeling
on the bed next to me. *Honey, I'm fine.*
Even blushed with bruises she looks good. She's lying.
Revenge too sweet attracts flies
in a blacked-out car park. My wife cries.
I know why. I'm three shots away from the parked car
put five holes in my daughter. I know who they are.
It's a week since they beat up my wife,
spewing up so much low life
it was biblical. The Thames sunk the promenade
that night, it rained so hard.

# 100 chars
monkey@puzzle

wen a mn opN fires hs wa 2 d top thN
loses all overnyt blastN hs 3rd eye W a
fulstop dat's nt tragDy

tragDy's d lot of d nvr-left-d-blocks Mr
Nobody whose pebble– lyf is intrrptd
b4 he hs d chnc 2 rise

he wz no tragic hero hitN glasses W d
bosses til hs tragic flaw or f8 md him
free-fall frm a hi plce

2 cordon off hs larger-thN lyf as f it
wr a sculpture on a pavement framed
W blk n yellO dntnta tape

no 666 disgraced bt lucifer w/o d angL
status bringN lyt 2 r lacklust lyfs W a
tweet or status ^date

since tradin widescreen 4 smallscreen
ment mor tym tweetN thN livN nt noing
he wz ritN hs own r.i.p.

ea bite-sized scene of hs soap opera
buzzed n beeped on r fons wen he broK
d speed limit on hs =o&o>

nt d boy frm dat estate hu gru ^ 2 hang
n d park nekN a dImNd wyt he'd
plucked frm d crnA shop shelf

bt king of d gym W mscles bustN ot hs
skin lk he wtd 2B oder thN d skin hu
let fings gt undR hs skin

lk d poison ivy rumour dat he knw w@
he didn't knw he knw bout a don hu
hung himself bt left no note

n evry1 knw hu couldn't kip frm tapping
w@ wz hapNg lk sum1 wz payin him
2 freezeframe r errday lyfs

so borin dat wen he went dwn on ll 4s
n d pub eatN crisps OTF brayN lk a
beast twas fri nyt ntrtanmt

nt hs vengeful invisibl h& sprayin ^ dat
cryptic triptych tag on d wall only he n
hs gang cd undrst&

nvr held h&s W d superfit wed W 2 kdz
>- armwrestler hu ended ^ runN 2 f@
W a thug 1s her hubby died

nt bad nuf 2B betrayd n stabbd n d bk
by a bro W a knife 4 a h&shake or shot
X-( n bed by hs bredren

nt set ^ by a relativ 2 do tym 4 a crime
he nvr did nor a sngl dad W 3 kdz *vin
2 death in a hi rise

nvr d psychopath n lust W hs sis unzippn
hs mum's womb 2C whr he came frm
thN cutting hs own sic lyf

no hero kisD by fortuN losing hs hed 2
a wmn nor king e10 frm d NcyD by d
tapeworms of hs rank pride

no-one laced hs \~!~/ 2 snap him face
dwn n d p%l or stuk d knife n d numba-
pL8 of everyone's bst m8

a nobody hu didn't C d hit n run reverse
Nstead of rev in2 his =o&o> cuttN his
suspense mid-sentence

his fon buzzN n beepN d pulse of our
dull predictiv lyfs long aftr d medics
pronouncd him past tense

# Animals!
## Mozilla Firefox

Love or money? Sex or the city?
You see that *trade* over there, too pretty

for his own bod, the one by the jukebox
surrounded by birds but eyeing up I, The Firefox?

Not the peacock, the rooster,
bronze, crimped red hair, crisp blue jeans. Used to

daydream about him. Freud says there's only two
kinds of dreams, daydreams and wet dreams. You

never knew that, did you? They don't call me
Mozilla Firefox for nothing, I should be

on *Mastermind*. Anyway, this cock
has a hen for each day of the week, body clock

set for dawn, sings like he owns the farmyard
and I, Mozilla Firefox, starred

in his dream last night. Well, I gatecrashed.
All in red I was, slappered and eyelashed

from too many bevvies at the King's Head.
I put the pink pound in the red.

Money? Bah handbag! Money can't buy you love,
William Shakespeare. Anyway, he was outside 'Dove

Cottage', feathering one of his hens,
you know, the one in the gold choker who pretends

to sing his backing vocals like she's number one
in his chart, like she holds the key to his kingdom come,

Poutalot, her name is, so I hid behind a tree.
Animals! Worse than *The Heath* for bugs and he clocked me

swatting a dragonfly. So I had to come out, so to speak.
I said, *I saw you on TV last week.*

*Never heard a man hit a note so hard!*
Flattery is the way to a man's heart.

He cocks his head, sings his eyes shut and I, The Fox,
have the cock in my throat, the most tuneful of cocks!

Well, he doesn't quite know how to react,
you wouldn't, would you. And Poutalot puts on this act

like I'm murdering him. Death and Love,
same thing, John Donne. Then he calls my bluff.

Tells me to tell *her* to put a stop in the fanfare
so I part my lips to speak and he flies up into the air

and wakes up sweating in his blue jeans.
I told you, only two kinds of dreams ...

Now here comes Poutalot in her Wonderbra
to make him think he's some kind of pop star

cos he drinks Champagne on the rocks.
And he's making like he never clocked The Firefox.

Chateau or cottage? Shop or shag?
Love? Bah, handbag!

# SITTINGBOURNE

# The Contract
Femme Fatale

Worst job I ever handled, bruv? A woman.
So plain, you'd scan her face for flaws, an find none.
Not a mark on her till the bullets spat.
They fucked up good, should be in here for that
not shelling Jupiter. Call this a prison!
Finishing school. He was never *christened*
Jupiter, but larged it, full of gas.
Jupiter Jones. One of his moons, I was.
He paid with interest, bruv, an when you got
a past, a job's a job. One thing I'm not
is lazy … She was sitting in the bath,
no bubbles, an so hot, I held my breath,
felt overdressed in t-shirt an tattoos.
*He wanted me to top myself*, she goes,
*but where's the fun in that?* Lilies, she smelt of,
so strong it made me gag. She eyed me, bruv,
the way all virgins eagle me but scanned
my lids too long, as if *I* killed her husband.
I never. Nor his brother. Not my business.
You never get a babe like that to kiss
Jupiter's arse: she laughed, gave him what for.
Not that he wanted *her*, he wanted her
to want *him*. But she fucked him with religion.
If there's one thing Jupiter hates, it's Christians.
He's killed more Christians than his wife's been headfucked.
I aim – and Lily-May's no longer perfect.
She doesn't flinch. Asks me to light her gold-
tipped cigarette. *Do you believe in God?*

I fire again, fuck the analysis.
Again! Who the fuck does she think she is?
And yet I'm answering: *No … I don't know.*
She blows smoke in my face. *I do*, she goes,
like nothing happened. Blood, fresh as graffiti,
the bath, the lino, deep in red confetti
and sister's singing Greatest Hits. I leave.
Took her three days to die. You don't believe
me, bruv? I shelled the boss and jacked it in,
buried the bullet, washed away the sin.
Only babe I ever killed, that kid,
I swear to God, worst job I ever did.
*I do*, she said, like we were hitched. I breathed
red roses, blubbered like a girl: believed.

# The Gold-Digger
Tim Canon-Yeo

Subspecies of suburbia
subtitled *The Twister*,
makar of mixed metals,
mercenary as mercury
my mastermixer.
Hidden in his hoodie
thinblack an' threadbare,
high as a horsefly he
goldplates the gangplank
from Backwards under Burbs
to Sin City centre.
Minted in his image I'm
alchemist's apprentice
craving this countercraft.
You want bling? I can blag it,
pale an' pocked as a planet
cos I don't do daylight
an' gold dust dulls me,
sweating like a sweatshop,
stench like a stinkstone
over a festering flame.
I've invested in a
one-way, no-win
gamble for glamchips,
dig for dolebuds in the dirt
recess of recession.
Come kiss the cauldron,
tip the mitt with quick silver

bling me the blingstone,
powder, piss, an' pepper.
Tweet The Twist mix the fix.
But a watched pot don't jackpot
so close yer lids, let
my master mix magic
fumes that mouth *Smoke me*.
Then crucible cracks,
nukes nega nuggets
an' chemicals choke me.
Exploding expletives,
I down tools, dare to
outmidas my master
and get the yo-heave-ho …
Fired, I'm fired up with
my master's master
the thought-fox of Fort Knox,
nickname *The Canon*,
godfather of gold.
So I counterfeit the mould,
don the don of a don,
an' become The Canon's convoy.
Come closer, come
watch the wordsmith wax
chemical cacophony,
lies laced with lucre.
Here pants a punter,
high priest of the high rise,
gangplank gangsta.
Croaks the cold Canon,
*Fetch me a fifty,*

*I'll ice you with interest.*
Canon keeps covenant,
pays back the payback
and gangsta's gagging for
the rags-rich recipe.
*Check me*, crows The Canon,
*master mix millions:*
*ground chalk to gold chain.*
*Kiss my Canon balls!*
Canon plants a nugget,
giltseed in coat sleeve.
Watch him switch the batch,
whitewash the black ash.
Abracadazzler …
*Gold!* groans the gangsta,
bling blinds the blinker.
Wants to whip the mix,
Canon flicks his wrist,
an' conjures more carats
that blink and bling *Bite me!*
They're fired as fireflies
higher than hi-fives …
I could tell a tale
how the horseman of hell
got a grand from the gangsta
for the rich quick mix
but this bard's behind bars,
my sentence is censored
an' gold dust dulls me.
But flick me a fifty
an' I'll twist my tongue

to craft a conclusion:
The Canon's a con
who's got it cold coming:
trick the trade you get tried,
gag The Guild you get *Guilty*,
fuck with fire you get fried.

# HARBLEDOWN

HARBLEDOWN

# The Crow
Scott Mansell

That night Pavel came to my house drunk.
*Angel*, he said, *Why is the crow black?*
*The crow?* I said, *What crow?* And he said,

Where I from like this. Small place. Is cold
but life good. I young, strong, I look good,
my hair is bright sun. Look at me now.
I play harp and sing like bird. No man
sing like I sing, no shoot like I shoot.
In the wood I read bird, sky like book.
I build house, kill pig, sell pig. Grow rich.
They say, he good man, work hard, clean heart.
I see girl black hair like you. Wild bird.
I love her. Put her gold ring in church,
put her on perch, feed her meat and drink.
    I work hard. Buy wife fine dress, red shoe,
fur coat. She cook, she clean. I pay maid.
My wife, she is my queen. I buy her
white bird for pet, white like snow-white swan.
It talk. It say my wife word, it sing
*Pavel!* to me, my name. It don't talk
to my wife, just me. *Pavel!* it sing.
    One day it rain bad, sky break in two.
I stop work, come home. My wife not there,
bird in cage talk. It sing, *I love you,*
*Yakov!* Not my name. Bird sing twice, *I*
*love you, Yakov!* My heart break in two.
My wife, my wild bird, eat worms in wood.

She come home. I don't talk. Her white bird
sing, *I love you, Yakov!* She go white.
I take knife and … she dead. I kill her.
Then I break harp, stab knife hard in chair.
The bird, it see all. I mad! My hair
fall out like snow, I will take my life.
My wife, my gem, she love me not him.
She lie dead, swan-white face. White bird lie!
I curse bird its tongue but curse come back.
When hair grow back, it black. I sleep bad,
I lose taste, sweet tongue, song. I see things,
bad things, I know when it storm and rain,
know when man die. Crow sit in my heart.

So I come here, small place. Make new start.
They say, he good man. No one know me.
You love me, Angel, you know is true.
Please not *say* you love me, cage your tongue
in teeth and lips. Your tongue, it cut love
in two. Cage your tongue, sweet, snow-white bird.
Put your hand here. My heart, it is wild.

# CANTERBURY

# The Gospel Truth

Rap, The Son aka 'The Parson'

*... Stand ye in the ways, and see, and ask for the old paths, where is the good way, and walk therein, and ye shall find rest for your souls ...*

– Jeremiah 6:16

*My beloved, truth isn't tender, it's tough.*
*I'm keepin it real, no rum, ram, ruf,*
*rhyme for a reason, reapin what it sows –*
*wheat not the chaff, punchier than prose.*
*So it flows – Seven Sins was my Crew, you can ask them,*
*use ta be 'The Pimp' but now I'm 'The Parson'.*
*Parental advisory, listen to the lesson,*
*this be no sermon, this be my confession ...*

Two roads diverged from the A2 –
one went to Heaven, the other *Hey, you!*
*Fancy some fun, brotha, won't ya park n ride?*
I paid a heavy price an I puckered up to PRIDE.
Her lips were wide, painted to a botox smile
and her scent more expensive than the square mile,
chandeliers in her ears and a designer outfit,
gown so long it was trailin in dogshit.
What of it? Sista had diamonds in her teeth,
the only thing concerned me was what was underneath ...
her bra was brief, her butt was big, the rapper drowned

in cleavage as full as the Dane John Mound.
Jack fell down and broke his crown for a bling singer,
diva wrapped the rapper round her ring finger.
I loved my enemy, vicar was the MC,
PRIDE was my bride and our bridesmaid was ENVY.

*Truth isn't tender, it's tough as they come,*
*keepin it real with a ruf, ram, rum.*
*Seven Sins was a rough an ready bunch,*
*my beloved, listen to the power of my punch.*

ENVY hung out with ASBOs and Chavs,
they was the have-nots and we was the haves.
She looked fine as a glass of wine but she craved
the high life, wanted to be my wife, slaved
in the kitchen creatin feasts to seduce me –
Whitstable oysters all tender and juicy.
Her tongue was forked, she was an ace cook
but she was bitchin us daily on Facebook
in French. She had a versatile tongue.
She gave me the rope and I was well hung.
She had two faces, one fair and one foul,
she had two brothers, fresh outta jail.
They were pimps – and she worked for them both,
the bad one was WRATH, and the mad one was SLOTH.
I took a stake in their undeclared business:
PRIDE was my bride and ENVY my mistress.

*Truth is tough when it comes to wham bam,*
*I hit the wrong road, the ruf, rum, ram.*
*Seven Sins was my Crew, I confess*
*but repentance is sweeter than a low-cut dress.*

WRATH and SLOTH were the Canterbury Krays,
suits so sharp you be bandaged up for days.
WRATH would attack if you said a crow was black,
SLOTH needed crack just to get out of the sack
an' I was Jack, plantin my cash to hatch gold.
But brothas was hatchin a plot to snatch tenfold,
sent sex on legs times two to unbutton me:
one was called GREED, the other called GLUTTONY.
They had a caterin business called Cayenne,
catered for men, if you know what I'm sayin
but they did weddings, and they managed mine,
GREED for the profit, GLUTTONY for fine wine.
GREED sucked the gold from my teeth till I was poor,
GLUTTONY ate my face till it was raw.
God's law, if you deal with deadly sins, you be dust …
that's what you get when PRIDE marries LUST.

*The gospel truth is a rough tough lesson*
*but hear me, beloved, here ends my confession.*
*In heart, in word, in deed I be repentin –*
*Canterb'ry Cathedral I be frequentin.*
*Took the wrong path but now I'm on the right track,*
*tempted but power of prayer helps me fight back.*
*Alright Jack, now that God is my guide,*
*Faith is my sista, Humility my bride.*

# Back Track (Grime Mix)
Harry 'Bells' Bailey

Now you've tuned to or leafed through this volume,
if you like any tales, tell the whole room!
If you slam this slam anthology,
for the sick bits, here's my apology:
to all Christians we misrepresented;
to all faiths that were nil represented;
for the hardcore macho and sexist,
every encore showing sex as sex *is*;
for the stereotypes, I hold my head low,
should I fix the mix? April said no,
keep the cursing, class A's and violence.
Our intent was to showcase this island's
love of retelling tales in its fierce pun
not to cut out the gem from its pierced tongue
so we're keeping it real on the papyrus:
all that's written is written to inspire us ...

# Author Biographies

**Mrs Alice Ebi Bafa:** I was born in Nigeria, married at 12 and lived in Ghana until Kwesi died. Then I married a man from Sierra Leone who died on our wedding night. Then I married an Englishman who died. Then a Nigerian who died also. My fifth husband is toyboy, live and kicking.

**Harry 'Bells' Bailey:** worked as bouncer when studying at London Guildhall Uni. Ended up managing pub. Now owns five London gastropubs, including legendary Tabard Inn in Southwark. There, hosts monthly storytelling night, *Plain Speaking*, which mixes live performance with Skype.
'London Bridge is dumbing down' *The Telegraph*
'High-brow meets Hi-tech' *The Guardian*

**Tim Canon-Yeo:** was born in Singapore but schooled in the UK. After obtaining a Medieval English degree from Oxford he was a TEFL tutor for several years in Colombia. Now he's a personal trainer and has been bodyguard to paranoid pop stars. He resides in Kent and writes a poem a day.

**Yves Depardon:** is a French-Canadian Professional Speaker and Business Coach living in Soho, Central London with his long-term partner. He's published 20 self-help books and six novels, including the multi-million best-seller, *Young, Free and Sinful* (Impress, 2007). He regularly uses poetry in his presentations. His 'love2Bme' lectures attract a 2,000-strong online audience.

**Missy Eglantine:** born St Lucia/raised in Lewisham/R&B singer-rapper-poet/recording debut album/training 2B lay preacher/studied French UEL Stratford/owns 3 greyhounds/ Love Peace & Justice/volunteer 4 RSPCA/just opened beauty salon Peckham/Nails Jewels & Curls/Life is busy!/1st collection *Excuse my French*/published by Salt 2010.

**Femme Fatale:** dark cabaret performer and per(form)ance poet. Owns Whitstable-based vintage clothes shop, *Second to None*, specialising in '40s and '50s era. A *film noir* aficionado with large private collection of DVDs and videos. Likes dead poets: W. H. Auden, Edna St Vincent Millay and Thom Gunn. Poetry must have strict constraints.

**Mozilla Firefox:** I'm the illegitimate offspring of The Brothers Johnson and the Sisters of Perpetual Indulgence. I was dragged up off the Old Kent Road, London. Poetry's my first love: we have an open relationship. I adore the heroic couplet but free verse is OK, as long as you're wearing adequate protection.

**Huw Fryer Jones:** is from Colwyn Bay, North Wales. Studied music at Liverpool and did busking whilst a student for beer money and to impress the ladies. Brilliant! A born matchmaker, he makes his living singing at weddings. His lyrics are romantic: his verse is comic. Has published a poetry pamphlet with Seren.

**Yejide Idowu-Clarke:** I am a poet and publisher of academic books, educated at Queen's College, Lagos. I read PPE, specialising in Philosophy, at Magdalen College, Oxford, gaining a First Class Honours. I completed my master's degree in Creative Writing at Oxford Brookes University in 2009. I am based in London and Lagos.

**Robert Knightley:** is Professor of Creative Writing at UEA, a poet who has represented the British Council in Egypt, Turkey, Lithuania, Russia, Spain, Morocco and Algeria. His work is translated into 15 languages. His third collection, *Truth, Honour, Freedom and Courtesy* (Carcanet Books, 2010), was shortlisted for the T S Eliot Prize.

**Frankie Lynn:** once upon a time, there was a wee girl who grew up in an open house with open books that opened minds. They grew their own food and ran a vegan cafe in Edinburgh, *Tatties and Neeps*, giving free food to the homeless. One day, she found a magic pen ...

**Scott Mansell:** My school report said 'Scott will end up famous or in prison'. I left school with no qualifications, went from runner to trader at London Stock Exchange. Learnt Russian at night school and specialised in Eastern Europe. Retired at 40. Married an English teacher and started writing as a hobby ...

**Soul Merchant:** was converted in Wigan Casino '74 and hasn't looked back. Became Northern Soul record dealer and for years ran massive stall in Affleck's Palace, Manchester. Specialised in rare imports, white labels. Been DJ for 20 years. Now has regular spot at the Twisted Wheel. This is his first published piece.

**Robyn Miller:** Bolshy big bi redhead. Taurus, Leo rising. Part-time barmaid, full-time motormouth. Likes performance poetry. Punk poets John Cooper Clarke, Joolz, Steve Tasane. Loves Luke Wright, Hollie McNish, Kate Tempest. Anything that packs a punch. Wrestles for relaxation. Hates glass ceilings, religious bigots, size 8 anything. Lives, drinks, fights in Deptford.

**monkey@puzzle:** creates crosswords and quizzes for national newspapers. The '100 chars' form came from Chaucer's intro to the 'Monk's Tale': '… first, tragedies wol I telle,/of which I have an hundred in my celle', and Carol Ann Duffy's quote: 'The poem is a form of texting … it's the original text.'

**Mel O'Brien:** was born in Belfast, raised in Chatham and teaches English at a secondary school in Gravesend, Kent. Her poem was inspired by *The Long Memory* (1953) starring John Mills, filmed in and around Gravesend. Also, Jonathan Nolan's short story, 'Memento Mori', that was later adapted for the film *Memento* (2000).

**Rap, The Son aka 'The Parson':** learnt my skills on the street not the classroom/African ancestry, spittin in my hands free/born, bred and battlin in Canterbury/Set an ex-sample to inspire you/ if gold rusts, what will iron do?/Fired by KRS-One and the Bible/in the hip hop academy, an Old Skool disciple.

**Ozymandia Reeves:** was expelled from school before she learnt to hate poetry. Taught herself Anglo-Saxon and got Medieval Studies MA from York University. Been professional carpenter for years. Was runner-up in Ilkley Literature Festival Competition 2010 and now working on first slim volume and audiobook. Originally from Norfolk, now lives in Leeds.

**Klaudia Schippmann:** was born in Bordeaux and schooled in Dartmouth, Devon. Inspired by the creative process of Alice Oswald's *Dart*, Schippmann often interviews her poetic subjects, attempting to replicate their speech in verse. 'Things' is a literary recreation of a conversation with a socialite on a BA flight from Hull to Cartagena.

**Memory Anesu Sergeant:** Originates from Zimbabwe. She practised for several years as a barrister specialising in land law and leases. However, she began writing seriously during maternity leave and completed her first collection, *Coat of Many Colours* (Bloodaxe, 2008). She learns her poems off by heart and reads regularly on BBC Radio 4.

**Dr Kiranjeet Singh:** Formerly a plastic surgeon with a passion for poetry, she now prefers to reconstruct lines on the page rather than the face. This piece was partly a response to the newspaper coverage of the beheading of Manju Kunwar in 2012; partly homage to the concrete poems of sculptor Carl Andre.

**Jeu'di Squires:** English & Cre8ive Writing wordsmith @ Goldsmiths. She wears the emporer's new clothes embroidered with red&white flowers. Jeu'di's learning the French horn & her fave read is *La Disparition* by Georges Perec. She intends to write her poetic thesis, *Hidden Love Letters*, in invisible ink only legible under UV light.

**Geoff Sumner:** left school at 16 to run fruit and veg stall in South London. Done every job you can think of, bailiff, used-car-dealer, door-to-door salesman. Now a stand-up who kills heckles with a couple of one-liners you won't print. Only drinks red wine. Likes doing poetry gigs, less money, more laughs.

**Sir Topaz & Da Elephant: ST**: I be born an' bred in East … **DE**: He was born in Islington and went to Cambridge … **ST**: Lies, lies … **DE**: The truth. We met at Cambridge, Baron Cohen gave a lecture … **ST**: We hooked up at Limehouse, bro. **DE**:… and created this double act … **ST**: 'Cept it's no act. **DE**: … because he hasn't got a girlfriend …

**Roger of Ware:** is the literary descendent of John Skelton, an in-yer-face spitter with an unsavoury crew, 'Too many Cooks', proving a man is only as good as the company he keeps; his infamous 'Roving Mic' events regularly divide intellectual audiences unsure whether it's acceptable postmodern irony or he really is a \*\*\*\*.

# Acknowledgements

Poems have appeared in versions in the following publications: 'Makar' and 'Things' in *The Edinburgh Review*; extracts of 'Roving Mic' in *In Their Own Words*; 'Joined-up Writing' in *Long Poem Magazine*; '~~Reconstruction~~' in *Magma*; 'The Crow' and 'The Gospel Truth' in *On the Line*; 'Unfinished Business' in *Poetry Review, The Best British Poetry 2012* and *Gravesend Reporter*; 'Emily', 'The Gold-Digger' and 'The Devil in Cardiff' in *Poetry Wales*; 'Sharps an Flats' in *Silk Road Review* (USA); 'What Do Women Like Bes?' in *Transformatrix* (as 'The Wife of Bafa').

Recordings of my readings of a number of these poems are available on the Poetry Archive – http://www.poetryarchive.org.

I would like to warmly thank Arts Council South East and the National Lottery for a generous Grant for the Arts and The Authors Foundation for a development bursary which enabled me to complete this book.

I would also like to thank the following friends, colleagues and organisations who have been enormously supportive of this project: everyone at Canongate, especially my editors Francis Bickmore, Vicki Rutherford and Helen Bleck; Professor Helen Cooper, Jeremy Clarke, Patricia Debney, Francesca Beard, Keiren Phelen, John Prebble, Rosie Turner, Vicky Wilson, Jane Draycott, Ros Barber, Jay Bernard, Jenny Lewis, Luke Wright, Apples &

Snakes, Dr Gail Ashton, Steve Tasane, Geoff Allnutt, Nina Tullar, Sarah Salway, Professor Peter Brown, Professor Bernard O'Donoghue, Henry Eliot, Tim Shortis, Julie Blake, Barbara Bleiman, Kate Clanchy, Trevor Eaton 'The Chaucer Man' and numerous audiences who have given me invaluable feedback.

Finally, I would like to thank Geoffrey Chaucer for creating a literary work that defies time and space.